D1567416

NEVER
STOP
DESIGNING
SPACES.

NEVER STOP DESIGNING SPACES.

An Emotional Journey
through Ten Places
of Italian Life

Daniele Lago

RIZZOLI
NEW YORK

New York · Paris · London · Milan

Art direction
BRH+

Project coordination
Stefano Locci

Graphic design
GVilla Design

Copywriting
Valentina Cavicchiolo
Virginio Briatore

Translation
Sarah Elizabeth Cree

Editing
Gail Swerling

Post production
Luce Group

Technical coordination
Sergio Daniotti
Cristina Scalabrini

First published in the United States of America in 2017
by Rizzoli International Publications, Inc.
300 Park Avenue South
New York, NY 10010
www.rizzoliusa.com

ISBN: 978-0-8478-4999-4

© 2016 Rizzoli Libri S.p.A./Rizzoli, Milan

All of the products in this volume were designed by Daniele Lago and his team, composed of Andrea Leoni, Andrea Pilotto, and Paola Brotto and LAGO STUDIO for LAGO.
The interiors project from which the images in this volume were drawn was supervised by Alessandro Corrò. The styling of same was handled by Lucia Tramarin, Make that Studio, and Paola Brotto.

2017 2018 2019 2020 / 10 9 8 7 6 5 4 3 2 1

Library Congress Control Number: 2016959408

Printed in Italy

THE JOURNEY

In Italy, people's lives play out at home, at cafés, and at hotels. They cook, they celebrate, and they meet at the office. It's life. A life where objects and people have been travelling, everywhere, from the beginning, nourishing a web of stories, knowledge, positive emotions, joy and, sometimes, pain. We move and we nourish beauty. The stupendous Italian beauty that the landscape, architecture, and art history have lent the present generation so that it can pass it on to the next one in good condition. An Italy that also needs to be relaunched, starting from the incredible biodiversity of the country, which has a cultural and artistic heritage unique in the world, associated with a community of people who sustain intense friendships and collaborations, in the cities as well as in the non-urban areas. As an Italian company that manufactures its products in Italy, we wanted to celebrate this richness with a journey through the 'culture of living' that we feel is special to our country, using our design to make a new contribution to the way interiors are conceived and lived.

"*NEVER STOP DESIGNING SPACES. An Emotional Journey through Ten Places of Italian Life*" is a highly imaginative "tour" of a series of Italian interiors from different periods and contexts. Each interior, domestic or otherwise, was set in a specific location, imagining an intense dialogue between furnishings, people, and contexts.

Our selection of the ten cities was inspired by Trivago's "Global Reputation Ranking 2016," which was based on best online reputation and identified the most interesting and contemporary places in Italy: Assisi, Matera, Sorrento, Naples, Lucca, San Vito Lo Capo, Vicenza, San Gimignano, Turin and Livigno. This ranking rewards the importance of content and passion, two aspects that we at LAGO pour into our furnishings and all of our interior projects, with the ambition of seeing our work recognised as a proud, successful representative of the excellence of Italian know-how.

Our home is the whole wide world and LAGO brings the world into the homes, hotels, B&Bs, private spaces and public places we live in. LAGO design is open to the influence of others' lives. It adapts to the solid walls of old houses and the huge windows of today's architecture, the mountain tradition and that of the sea, frequent moves and time-defying stays.

LAGO design is energy, modularity, solidity, business opportunity, and life opportunity. And then there is the design that might be for LAGO the most important of all, the one that does not exist yet. The one that we need to create together, me, you, us. A concept of future that still needs to be built, listening to each other. Tomorrow's journey. The place not yet seen.

Daniele Lago

LAGO INTERIOR LIFE Manifesto

The LAGO INTERIOR LIFE philosophy is encapsulated in an 11-point manifesto that outlines its key elements. Point 6 is empty, because we are always in a state of becoming and it is in the void that we create, learn, and write, every day, our own lives.

#1   Immediate and simple.

#2   We design interiors for your interior life.

#3   We believe in the atoms and bits of human relationships.

#4   We have a compass—Head Heart Courage.

#5   We plan the solid to breathe life into the void.

#6   ....

#7   Beauty lies in the vision of the whole.

#8   The essentials, for enduring over time.

#9   You are the design; we provide the alphabet.

#10   Creativity comes when you do what you love.

#11   Never stop.

INDEX

ASSISI

NEVER STOP LIVING GRACEFULLY.

Assisi | Umbria
43° 04' 12" N
12° 37' 03" E

A place of spirituality and brotherhood. The land of Saint
Francis and Saint Clare, spreading over the green hills
of Umbria, filled with sharply defined stone buildings
that hide frescoes and other masterpieces inside. A mix
of old hamlets, chests filled with art and visions, local
architecture covering the sloping hills, the strong flavors
of the countryside, the colors of bread and earth, ceramic
and cool rivers. Raw, durable fabrics, warm in winter,
cool in summer.

Sometimes the living room of modern homes becomes an office where you can get work done undisturbed.

In the lush natural surroundings of Assisi, harmony is everywhere: in the song of the birds that greet the day, in the fragrance of the damp earth, in the sun filtering through the leaves of the trees. Immersed in these green woods, you enter into communion with the cosmos and, through the essential, reach the place where the soul resides. The same suspended atmosphere is sought out in the place where everyday life unfolds, through an elegance that transcends trends and is measured in the passage of time over the course of a lifetime. The interior of this private apartment is built on tranquil tones, with colors drawn from Assisi's natural surroundings. The rigor of the design is broken up by the unusual, modular shape of the Slide sofa and the Slide floor. The suspension of the furnishings is intensified by the transparency of the glass: from the 36e8® Glass containers and the Air bookshelf, to the Air sideboard, everything seems to float in the air. The new round Air table in glossy glass is a gathering point that brings together both architecture and people, joyfully welcoming diners and the feast with its balanced, perfect shape.

A revolutionary
square module
stands at the
base of a flexible,
customizable
system.

Use the little to build the big. Designed by Daniele Lago, 36e8® is a system of modular containers that anyone can design to fit the spaces of their own home and to meet their own personal needs. The modules are generated by a basic square 36.8 cm/side and by its multiples and submultiples. 36e8® guarantees extreme compositional flexibility, freedom of form, and certainty of content. 36e8® Glass is an all-glass container that creates effects of surprising lightness and transparency.

Magical suspension: the bookshelf seems to float in the air, while light and landscape filter inside.

The aerial structure of the Air shelf enhances the luminosity of the room, providing a view of tranquil Assisi, perched on the slopes of Monte Subasio, which gave the city pink stone for its churches, bell towers, and public squares. To conceive the Air system, Daniele Lago inverted the order of the factors, giving the supporting structures in transparent glass extreme lightness, and the shelves and containers weighty physicality. The result is a two-faced shelf that seems to float in the air. It can also be set up in the middle of the room to divide any living spaces in an aerial and elegant way, while at the same time creating lots of space for keeping books and other items.

A welcoming and comfortable sofa is born from the Slide modular system: a rectangle cut in two by an oblique line, generating two trapezoid-shaped modules which become seats and seat backs. Loads of compositional freedom, fabrics that are soft to the touch and a mix of technology, artisan know-how and creativity.

"I was in Assisi: it is a wonderful thing, land, city, and sanctuary, for those who understand nature and art in their harmony with history, imagination, and human affection."

Giosue Carducci

The incredible flexibility of the Air system has
given shape to an elegant sideboard, distinct
for its essential, timeless design. The glass sheets
that support the containers disappear and the
volumes seem to magically float in the air.

Soft shape, surprising suspension.

Suspended on invisible glass legs, the round Air table seems like a disk floating in the air. Its circular shape creates a welcoming atmosphere in the home, fostering conversation and sharing. The sinuous, essential lines find solidity in the table top, which conceals the fastening system and results from attention paid down to the smallest detail.

MATERA

NEVER STOP BEING EVER-CHANGING.

Matera | Basilicata
40° 40' N
16° 36' E

Matera, with its singular and unmistakable architecture,
is a labyrinth of rock where the ingenuity of humankind
has successfully blended itself with the natural
environment. In the City of Rocks, European Capital of
Culture 2019, at once both prehistoric and contemporary,
rock churches and art galleries meet in one of the oldest
settled places in the world. About this gem, a UNESCO
World Heritage Site, Lucio Dalla wrote: "The uniqueness
of Matera is a miracle of time, a happy harmony
between history and contemporary life."

Let yourself be charmed by the old fascination of Matera and lose yourself among the little lanes that tell of its millennial history, sculpted in the rock. Treat yourself to long tranquil breaks, filled with silence and equilibrium. Let yourself be cradled by a luxury made up of atmosphere, privacy, and pleasure. Rediscover the same sensations in the harmonies of a design that celebrates the quality of everyday life. In a setting that picks up the colors of sunny Matera, the Air island kitchen gives exchanges between people a starring role. Suspended on transparent glass legs, and with an induction hob, it fosters dialogue between those who cook and those who participate in the magic rituality of food preparation, both visually and through vicinity to the cook. The Air kitchen, winner of Salone del Mobile.Milano award 2016, was designed by Daniele Lago. It can be paired with the 36e8® kitchen system and is completed by a wall-mounted pantry with built in appliances, creating a strikingly clean look.

The kitchen and the table can be a single entity, since together is better.

The circularity of the Air kitchen lends fluidity to social encounters, whether special occasions or the everyday.

The space picks up the colors and architecture of Matera through geometric overlapping that changes with the light, whether natural or artificial. The dynamic of the corner, which recalls the houses perched on the rock, is amplified, creating the sensation of a transition underway. From the furnishings, vast fields of color extend on the wall like the shadows of the houses, which change with the variations of light during the day. The colorful planes alternate with more rhythmic patterns that trigger a dialogue of strong perceptive divergences. In this interior, the 36e8® Side kitchen with a glass countertop and dark, contrasting Wildwood doors, the 36e8® larder and the 36e8® Glass containers are all suspended on the wall. The round Air kitchen adds an element of softness that rounds the corners and fosters empathy and conviviality.

"It's not that I love Matera, but that I found the cosmic roots of mankind there."
José Ortega

The 36e8® Column was developed out of the 36e8® system; this suspended larder is the natural complement to the 36e8® kitchen. The interior glass shelves add lightness to the structure, and they can accommodate built-in appliances.

The glass offers a new experience of color, which becomes dynamic, profound, and changeable with the variations of light.

In the 36e8® Wildwood kitchen the Wildwood
fronts pair old oak with a 6-mm thick aluminum
profile providing protection and support.
The glass countertop integrates the washbasin
and the hob, while the dishwasher is suspended,
for better ergonomics. An almost invisible mark on
the door acts as a handle that, with a simple touch,
retracts and makes it easier to open cupboards.

**The Sassi–ancient cave dwellings–
are the oldest part of the city.
Visitors walking along their
narrow lanes and up their steep
stairs are treated to picturesque
views at every corner.**

SORRENTO

NEVER STOP FEELING MEDITERRANEO.

Sorrento | Campania
40° 37' 40" N
14° 22' 25" E

This city is like a terrace onto the sea, offering a bright
palette of color, flowers, and lemons: 2,500 years
of history set like a jewel in the blue waters of the Gulf
of Naples. Healthy, strong flavors, authentic cuisine,
where the countryside meets the sea and pasta is served
with fish. The powerful, vital light filters through the
curtains and shutters during the day, while the airy
evenings are long and perfect for enjoying with family
and friends.

**In the summer
residence, the living
room and kitchen have
an open-space plan to
maximize enjoyment.**

The colors of the interior and the furnishings echo the typical features of the Mediterranean landscape: sand, sea, white rocks. It is a convivial room that welcomes both kitchen and living room, transmitting the gift for hospitality that has been passed down in Sorrento for generations. It is a sunny, open house with a large window for watching the changing colors of the sea and sky every hour of the day. The kitchen, central to life in southern Italy, has an unstructured peninsula supported by glass; it is covered with hand-painted ceramic MadeTerraneo tiles, which make it unique and unmistakable

with their time-honored practicality and bring the warm hues of the south to the room. In the living area, a modular Air sofa and the Air Wildwood table rest on invisible glass supports, and contribute to recreating the sense of lightness that you feel when listening to the sound of the waves breaking on the beach. The 36e8® wall composition in the living area picks up the colors of the kitchen, while the MadeTerraneo hand-made ceramic tiles create a shelf with a jagged edge, like the cliffs of the Sorrento coast.

Hand-painted ceramic becomes an innovative little module for decorating kitchen islands and peninsulas.

People gather in the kitchen, the beating heart of every southern Italian home, to savor the aromas and flavors of this rich and fertile land: the delicate freshness of citrus, the pervasive intensity of aromatic herbs, the juicy fragrance of tomatoes. Meals are prepared working on a counter covered in hand-painted ceramic borrowed from the Mediterranean tradition. The kitchen brings together old materials and innovative uses. The hand-painted ceramic tile, a product typical of southern Italy, becomes the base module for the top and peninsula that, like a gigantic pixel in irregular configurations, gives movement and color to the kitchen. The 36e8® MadeTerraneo kitchen peninsula is suspended on glass legs and it seems to float in the air.

Artisan methods and attention to detail, even the ones most hidden.

Accessories, which are often hidden and the exclusive domain of the chef of the house, are what complete innovative kitchen systems like that of the 36e8® kitchen. They not only respond effectively to the chef's organizational needs and the actual activity of cooking, but also make it all special through surprising ergonomic solutions.

"Sorrento is a city of unspeakable beauty, deep poetry, voluptuous charm—and even serenity."

Matilde Serao

The first suspended modular sofa to configure and reconfigure in space and time.

The Air sofa system, designed by Daniele Lago, is a spatial and aesthetic revolution, and it finds its real strength in its ability to be transformed. The backrests and seats are completely interchangeable, so the sofa can be given a new look at any time. Lots of attention has been poured into ergonomics and selecting sustainable materials and processes. The glass legs transform the sofa into something ethereal, lightening up the room.

The Air shelf is dressed up in the colors of the Mediterranean, thanks to its hand-painted ceramic surface, the modules for which can be arranged in irregular shapes. It includes all of the colors of that flowering garden we know as Sorrento: the blue of the Mediterranean, the green of the maquis, the red of ripe tomatoes, and the dazzling white of the houses gleaming under the southern Italian sun.

Hundred-year-old wood suspended in mid-air has a soul full of life to be told.

Warm and light, the Air Wildwood table is made up of a time-worn oak top set on transparent glass legs. The wood grain tells the story of the life that flows around it, the stories of this city, where music can be heard at every corner, in the voices of children shouting and women chatting from one house to the next. By integrating an audio system and wireless charging into its surface, Daniele Lago designed a brand new version of the Air Wildwood table, that can play music and recharge smartphones: the Air Sound Table.

In the gardens, the air is filled with the fragrance of the Femminiello Sorrentino, a lemon that only grows here and flavors local cuisine.

NAPOLI

NEVER STOP ADMIRING BEAUTY.

Napoli | Campania
40° 50' N
14° 15' E

Naples is a hotbed of emotions. Chaos and order,
faith and reason. A wealth of history, color, and
human warmth. Music and culture in the heart of the
Mediterranean. The houses are wrapped in light, the old
welcomes the new, the statues stand out on the churches
and buildings, and the Baroque friezes and gold are
reflected in the perennial clarity of the sea horizon.

Timeless design for dreaming while suspended in the eternal beauty of a late eighteenth-century residence.

Walking in the shadow of Mount Vesuvius, through the packed streets of a city, where the splendors of the past left behind an immense artistic heritage, transports you to a place outside time. Here, tradition integrates perfectly with modernity, making Naples an intricate weave of historical and archaeological layers. The same timeless atmosphere, suspended between the ancient and the modern, also permeates this private late eighteenth-century residence. White walls with plaster stucco decoration and a herringbone wooden floor define an interior where just a few basic elements have been chosen with discretion to integrate with the pre-existing context: a Fluttua bed, a Duee wardrobe, and the round Wildwood bedside tables, completed with a generous Air sofa suspended on glass legs and a LagoLinea bookshelf with a geometric, modular design that recalls an ancient Greek frieze. This is the syncretism of Naples, a mysterious, fascinating city, where good taste is the norm and cultural life is found in both literary cafés and the lively local markets. Hospitality is a cult, there's always room for a friend or relative, travel is part of the game and everyone is always both near and far.

The light in Naples is blinding, but you can find respite under the colonnade of the main cloister of the Certosa di San Martino, a splendid example of seventeenth-century Neapolitan architecture.

The two volumes seem to be nested one inside the other like an embrace, like the two souls of Naples, one dark, the other light, that co-exist side-by-side, making this city enigmatic, fatalistic, and contradictory. This is the play of volumes you find in the Duee wardrobe, which seems to be magically floating in the air, thanks to the LED lighting and to the suspension of the internal volume. In reality, the door of the external volume extends beyond one end, creating a niche that can be fitted out with hangers and shelves.

A single 3 cm line for creating bookshelves in any shape you like on the wall.

Point, line, surface. LagoLinea has revolutionized the concept of the static grid bookshelf, allowing the creation of figurative or classical outlines, starting from a single line, 3 cm thick. The slenderness of the shelving makes it possible to suspend it from its sides, eliminating the structural constraints that limit expressive capacity. This way, you can create extremely customized bookshelves, always characterized by extreme lightness, from repeating modular patterns or shapes that conjure up animals and plants to linear and grid compositions.

"See Naples and die."

J.W. Goethe

Placed in a setting inspired by Neoclassical Naples, the Air MadeTerraneo table is simultaneously both a basic and a characterizing element. The transparent glass legs disappear, giving center stage to the ceramic top, decorated by hand in the warm, tranquil tones of terracotta. The de-structured form innovates the traditional perception of the table. In Naples, the art of ceramics achieved excellence and reached its apex in Capodimonte china, but also in ceramic church floors, cloister decoration, and the majolica revetment of domes and bell towers.

NEVER STOP CHANGING TASTE.

Lucca | Toscana
43° 51' N
10° 31' E

Famed for its 100 churches, its more than 4-kilometer-long circular Renaissance wall, and its elliptical Piazza dell'Anfiteatro, this is one of the best preserved art cities in Europe, where everything is on a human scale.
An ideal city, a perfect circle, where people get around on foot or by bike, and find the time to linger in its piazzas, church squares, gardens, cafés, restaurants, and markets.

The pleasure of feeling at home, even at the osteria.

In Lucca, the air is filled with love for, and the cult of, music, not just that of Puccini, which can be enjoyed in the many theaters and auditoriums scattered throughout the city and its environs, but also the music that can be heard in the city's little lanes and public squares, its churches and its luthiers' workshops. Musical notes also reverberate in this gourmet osteria with a 1950s feel, set up in a renovated post-industrial factory. It is a space that serves business and pleasure, a place for refreshment and gathering that fosters conversation and intimacy. The 36e8® kitchen is the center of activity, with its warm Wildwood doors and a countertop that combines Wildwood and Steel+, the new finish with a brushed surface incised with subtle marks that create the suggestion of wooden planks. These marks humanize the steel, giving warmth to a material that is faultless in technical terms, but usually perceived as cold. The kitchen is completed by two N.O.W. larders, opposite of which are small square MadeTerraneo tables and Steps chairs. Contemporary spaces for new urban needs, for getting together in person and connecting live.

"Everything in Lucca looks like it is in perspective. This is not one of those cities that can be taken by surprise, from the back."

Edith Wharton

Suspended on invisible glass legs, the 36e8®
Steel+ kitchen transmits an immediate sense
of warmth and welcome, the same that visitors
experience when arriving in Lucca to discover
its ancient beauty or the pilgrims who come
there along the Via Francigena. The kitchen's
Wildwood countertop and doors are a perfect
complement to the countertop in Steel+,
the brushed stainless steel surface of which
features fine etched lines that resemble wooden
slats. These subtle lines give rhythm and life
to the finish, which of course still preserves
all of its technical characteristics intact.

The contrast between
Wildwood and Steel+ enhances
the intrinsic qualities of the
two fine materials, which find
perfect harmony in the 36e8®
Steel+ kitchen.

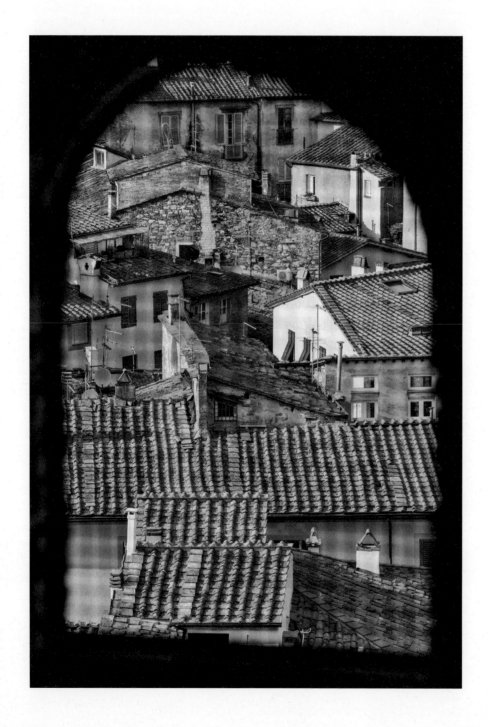

SAN VITO LO CAPO

NEVER STOP GOING NATURAL.

San Vito Lo Capo | Sicilia
38° 10' N
12° 45' E

Located on the northwest point of Sicily, the long white sand beach of San Vito Lo Capo and the neighboring pebble beach, the small "Spiaggia del Bue Marino," have long been considered among the most beautiful in Italy. They inspire a desire for a place that is relaxing, warm and natural, friendly and pure; this little town, dotted with low fishermen's houses, a cultural crossroads, the Caribbean pearl of the Mediterranean, is a dream come true.

Immersed in pristine nature, at a resort surrounded by the sea.

The crystalline water, velvety sand, and enveloping perfume of flowering juniper make San Vito Lo Capo an earthly paradise. In this peaceful little town of clear, intense colors, you can discover Sicily at its most authentic, offered intact to delight the eyes of visitors seeking out tranquility and rest. At this resort, located just steps from the sea, the area dedicated to care for the body is built around hues that recall Mediterranean scrub. A large window lets in the fresh air and scent of the sea, while soft light filters in through woven bamboo panels. The furnishings are minimal to keep the focus on immersion in nature, the interior palette picking up its hues. A Cellule washbasin conjures up the simplicity of small troughs carved out of stone, a LagoLinea composition with a 36e8® mirror and a Soft Bench seat create a little corner of wellness far from the world, transporting us to a pristine, wild setting.

**The tall tower of the
lighthouse of San Vito
Lo Capo is 40 meters high.
At night, its sabre of light
guides sailors away from
the rocky shallows.**

The perfection of the circle. Nothing more.
So much from so little. A freestanding circular basin
made of Cristalplant®, around which you can
arrange, like little cells, Wildwood or colored glass
trays and metal towel holders.

VICENZA

NEVER STOP BEING PALLADIO.

Vicenza | Veneto
45° 33' N
11° 33' E

The aristocratic urban houses and residential villas
in the environs, designed by the great architect
Andrea Palladio in the sixteenth century, give the area
of Vicenza an unmistakable appearance. The art
of living well and openness are at home here, along
with masterful execution and attention to detail.
The gentle hills of the Colli Berici embrace the city
on one side, offering tourists a landscape filled with
picturesque views and architectural wonders set in
an unspoiled natural oasis.

A hotel in a sixteenth-century building where art, design, and architecture meet.

As Palladio himself declared: "The height of civilization is achieved through perfect agreement with nature," which he himself masterfully achieved in the design of villas that perfectly integrate with the surrounding natural landscape. His genius also permeates the elegant historical center of Vicenza, and accompanies visitors walking along Corso Palladio, among loggias and porticoes, statues and colonnettes, up to the Teatro Olimpico, one of his greatest masterpieces. The sense of good taste and Vicenza nobility is also well expressed in this hotel guest room. The colors of the furnishings pick up the hues of the frescoed walls, while the glass supports of the suspended Air Wildwood bed and Air Storage enhance the terrazzo floor, a decorative element that is also a local specialty. The setting is completed by a N.O.W. wardrobe in the Gentle variation and a Chama armchair that transforms into a bed with a simple gesture. The adjacent bathroom expresses the same harmony between classical and modern, with powder-hued Morgana storage, and a Wildwood Depth washbasin, functional sculptures of the present.

The surprising lightness of Air, created with
semi-invisible sheets of crystal glass on which
the units rest, projects the dressing-table directly
onto a cloud, creating an unrivaled and
spectacular effect.

Fall asleep suspended in the air, resting your head on the trunk of a tree.

The Air Wildwood bed combines the transparency of glass with the warmth of wood. The texture of the Wildwood finish exalts the natural grain of the wood and shows the signs of wear and the passage of time. This is wood that has lived, where imperfections and marks give the product its true added value. Fabric-covered accessories that can serve as side tables and object containers can be attached anywhere along the headboard.

Wardrobes without handles, that become part of the architecture of the room.

The colors of the wardrobe pick up the white marble of Vicenza palazzos. Strong formal cleanliness and the lack of handles almost make it part of the architecture of the room, reducing the perception of bulk. Traditional doors step aside for glass panels of various dimensions that can be customized in size and color, which lend lightness, rhythm, and depth to the room. Modular, it adapts to both spaces and needs.

Natural, innovative materials create a harmonious space dedicated to reinvigoration and refreshment.

A window on the earth, a window on water. The result of a subtraction of volumes from an 8-cm-thick shelf, Depth is a washbasin that plays with our sense of void and depth. The transparent glass bottom changes our perception of the ritual of daily personal care, treating us to a surprising experience. It is like standing in front of an ancient spring in the green woods of the Colli Berici.

SAN GIMIGNANO

NEVER STOP BEING KIDS.

San Gimignano | Toscana
43° 28' N
11° 03' E

In the year 1300, this town had seventy-two towers. Today, only fifteen remain, but the thirteenth/fourteenth century appearance that crystallized there over the centuries makes it one of the best examples in Europe of the city planning of its time. This medieval Manhattan makes you want to play with history, scale the towers, and get a bird's-eye view of the undulating hills stretching to the horizon.

The bed is up in a tree, little ones dream up worlds and grown-ups become kids again.

It feels like staying in one of San Gimignano's fifteen tower houses, with red-brick walls and wooden floors. These medieval skyscrapers dominate the skyline in this magical, surreal city, where time seems to have stopped in the Middle Ages. The children's room is designed to stimulate the imagination and exploration. Here, the quality is total: the furnishings are made to last out of fine materials, like the Wildwood used for the desk. The suspended LagoLinea Weightless bed is a tree house for going on incredible adventures, and the suspension creates a space for a second bed below. The LagoLinea bookshelf is shaped like a flamingo, and the whole room was designed to inspire the imagination, so that the mind can grow free and fertile.

"We went on a trip to beautiful San Gimignano, that noble city, high and turreted… the streets of this city are long and broad, it stands on a hill that embraces many others. It has many towers, which stand extremely high off the ground, and a bell tower that might be 20 ells…"

Michelangelo Buonarroti il Giovane

TORINO

NEVER STOP MIXING PAST AND FUTURE.

Torino | Piemonte
45° 04' N
7° 42' E

The first Italian capital. A city of rivers, mountains, and hills, aristocratic and industrial, Roman and Savoy, the poster child for Art Nouveau and historical cafés, and center of contemporary art. A new melting pot of ethnicities and cultures, Turin is transforming from its historical identity as the city of cars into a city of culture, higher education, and economic and social innovation. In addition to the royal residences, the reigning dynasties left Turin palaces and castles of inestimable value, like the Reggia di Venaria Reale, which, returned to its original magnificence after a long restoration, now hosts exhibitions and concerts.

At the cultural association, the time is always right for discussing and debating ideas, past and future.

Built on the banks of the Po River, Turin is a city with a thousand faces, a magical and sumptuous place that offers tourists a dynamic cultural life, found in its historical cafés, literary associations, museums, and art galleries. In the prestigious setting of this cultural association, set up in a seventeenth-century palazzo, the contemporary furnishings serve as a contrasting element, creating an intriguing marriage between ancient and modern. Container and contained are placed in dialogue, transmitting a home-like atmosphere that inspires conversation and relationships. Four tables, including the new round Air Wildwood table and majolica MadeTerraneo tables, are available for private meetings or gatherings. A LagoLinea shelf with a geometric design runs along the wall, organizing the complexity of life while making room for play and irony.

At the Royal Church
of San Lorenzo, when
you look up at the big
windows of Guarini's
bold dome from below,
they create what the
locals ironically call
the "face of the devil."

*"Wonderful clarity,
autumn colors, an
exquisite feeling of
well-being spreading
over all things."*
Friedrich Nietzsche

The cradle of the Risorgimento, Turin is a city with an intense social life, one that both looks inward and is open to outside influences. Around the tables of its cafés, relationships have formed and decisions have been made that changed the fate of Italy. The perfect shape for sharing ideas and projects, the round Air table fosters conversation and sharing. The tactile Wildwood top is a counterpoint to the transparency of the glass supports, and the table seems to float in the air.

Old wood: the grain holds within it the stories of the life that flows around it.

NEVER STOP SEEKING SERENITY.

Livigno | Lombardia
46° 32' N
10° 08' E

Built 1,816 meters above sea level, in the uplands
of the Alps, it has the largest population of all of Italy's
high-altitude cities, which is why it is also called Little
Tibet. It is a straightforward, isolated place, made up
of nature and frontier, trade, and silence. Few live there,
many pass through, drawn by the mountains, winter
sports, and summer hikes. Here, nature is powerful,
hospitality is fundamental, and the interiors are protective
and welcoming.

The chalet's bedroom smells like the woods and the wardrobe is surprisingly soft to the touch.

The people of Livigno love the stunning mountains that surround their little town, nestled in the biggest valley of Alta Valtellina, and they also love the crowds of tourists who come there every summer and winter. Livigno welcomes visitors with an international atmosphere that combines Italian, Swiss, and Austrian influences. It is a warm, comfortable vibe, just like the one in the bedroom of this chalet. The interior is welcoming and designed around tactile materials like wood and fabric. As is typical of mountain architecture, the walls are covered with wood, warming the room and echoed in the Wildwood of the 36e8® Side sideboard mounted on the wall. A large Et Voilà wardrobe fills the back wall, while a smaller wardrobe, with Tree clothes hangers and transparent glass shelves, is tucked into the upper level. The Vele bed has a fabric headboard that replaces the bedside tables, offering plenty of surface space for keeping your things. When it is nice outside, it is best to get out and experience the mountains, but if it rains or snows, it is a pleasure to stay inside, on the line between past and present.

Working with wool is a local specialty. In the past, the wool from this area was sold at the markets that supplied the wool mills of the Venetian Republic. Fabric is a popular decorative material for Livigno interiors, because of the warmth it brings to the home. Designed by Daniele Lago, the Et Voilà wardrobe integrates it as a structural and aesthetic element, eliminating what seemed inescapably essential: the door. Taut fabric closes the volumes, completely doing away with the perception of doors and surprising us when it reveals, with a simple gesture, the ample spaces inside. Et Voilà almost seems like a magic box with an indefinite surface. The optical illusion is accentuated by the fact that the fabric can cover infinite surfaces and blend in with the architecture of the room. Inside it, the Et Voilà Tree wardrobe is accessorized with shelves and drawers and with a metal rotating clothes hanger tree. By adjusting the height of the tree junctions and the rotation of the branches, you can optimize space.

A warm, fabric
wardrobe that
opens with a
single gesture.

Wood is another material that the people of Livigno have been working with for generations. Found in every home, it brings unsurpassable warmth to the room, like the 36e8® Side sideboard, designed by LAGO with doors in Wildwood, a 200-year-old wood that smells of life and stories waiting to be told. The sides of the 36e8® containers can be customized in different colors, offering a new avenue for personal expression in the interior.

The centuries-old forests
of Livigno grow slowly,
but they are generous
and provide the wood
that people have
been using from time
immemorial to build
their own homes.

Three panels, covered in fabric or leather, form the headboard of a warm and welcoming bed conceived to be a help for the way we live now. Designed by Andrea Leoni, Vele has lots of space for holding all kinds of objects: books, cups, cellphones, and romantic secrets; everything within arm's reach.

HEAD, HEART AND COURAGE

Life is an experiment carried out through a journey.
One of my companions on this extraordinary journey, whom
I first met years and years ago, has been "Design," a discipline
that LAGO sees above all as a tool for social transformation.
Design carries within it the potential to generate meaning, which
is in turn propagated through "bodies" produced and planned
with all the love in the world, which, through the centrality of
culture and the individual, leads us to work together to generate
beauty. A beauty supported by a form of social responsibility
that strives to maintain a balance between Head, Heart, and
Courage. I have always thought that the artist and the creative
process are more interesting than the work produced in and of
itself, which is why we created a beautiful place for living and
working that respects the fingertips that shape our products each
and every day. This place is the LAGO FACTORY, a building
designed around people and not vice versa: 11,000 square
meters, surrounded by greenery, filled with sunsets and light
that filter in through its transparent glass walls. At LAGO, every
gesture made throughout the entire process tries to create a
collective symphony, so that the orchestra can play in harmony
and the products it creates can express only exceptionality,
thanks to our true passion for what we do. We are a company
that tries to keep the social interests of everyone in mind, aware
that the individual who consumes is also the individual who
produces. We understood that an "un-factory" is not enough
to generate a meaningful brand and we envisioned how Design
could have a positive impact on the planet. In a world where
artificial intelligence is doing a lot of today's work,
we understood that empathy would have an increasing influence
on our future. That is why we conceived of our Design as
an alphabet that can be freely composed by anyone in order
to express themselves. Design that empathetically resonates
with living spaces and the people who live in them, making
everyone feel included. Starting from these premises, we then
envisioned a network that would mix physical places and digital
communities, spaces and people, and we called it the LAGO
INTERIOR LIFE NETWORK. This vast network connects millions
of people through the digital community and the dynamic spaces
that we design. Each one of them will experience our spaces
taking away a piece of this positive change. We have come to
think that what happens around objects is more important than
the objects themselves. That is why the LAGO INTERIOR LIFE
NETWORK is a project that connects houses, offices, hotels, etc.
with the aim of positively improving the world, partly through
the economy but also much more. It is a network of relationships
for sharing emotions and experiences and that can be used to
improve ourselves in every direction. NEVER STOP. is the seed
that generated this journey and aims to be an anthem to the
beauty of life, a call to live it to the fullest and to discover one's
own creative potential, seeking out what we were born to do
and sharing it with others, making our own contribution to the
world. It is an invitation to discover the power of starting again
and always, always seeing a future.

Daniele Lago, CEO and Head of Design of LAGO

PHOTOGRAPHY CREDITS

Printed in November 2016 by Errestampa S.r.l. – Orio al Serio (Bergamo)